HANDBOOK FOR

WHEELCHAIR LIFE

David Thulin

ISBN: 1479388505

ISBN 13: 9781479388509

Library of Congress Control Number: 2012918017
CreateSpace, North Charleston, SC

As I awoke from my coma, I awoke into a new reality. A reality where I needed a wheelchair to move. Since that day, I have learned much that I wish I knew earlier. This is my attempt to present that knowledge. Some of these tips may be irrelevant or wrong for you, but hopefully the tips can ease your transition.

- Do dips. If you do only one thing, let it be dips.

- Learn to, if you can, operate the wheelchair yourself.

- Almost daily, new and cool wheelchairs are invented. Keep your eyes peeled.

- Sometimes, walking again is simply not in the cards. Eventually, you will want it the same way that walkers want to fly.

- Everyone will want to help you with everything. Do not accept. Do it yourself.

- Get reasonably comfortable. Training will be hard if you are in pain. Spending time searching for ultimate comfort is often wasted.

- Try to get involved in the making of your food. Even if that means just looking.

- Wear a hat when out in the sun. And sunglasses.

- The wheelchair is for transport. Watch TV from the couch.

- Your wheelchair is not your prison.

- A light wheelchair is a good wheelchair.

- The best cushion might need to be broken in.

- It gets better.

- Have an extra set of wheels.

- Have at least one extra cushion.

- A narrow chair is a good chair.

- Train your shoulders. Often.

- Just try.

- No rush.

- Live the best life possible with the abilities you have today. Don't wait for tomorrow's abilities.

- Know that your unique toilet problem has a solution. Trust me.

- Head movement, when moving to and from your wheelchair, is vital. It weighs more than you think, and used correctly, it does half the work for you.

- Have a specialist make your wheelchair custom fit you. It makes a difference.

- If you do not want to dance, you have a perfect excuse. If you do, you will be the center of attention.

- Visit Southeast Asia. There, a wheelchair is not a problem.

- The type of pants you wear matters. Slippery pants are good for sliding back and forward.

- Learn to play chess. Well.

- Put something that reflects light on your jacket when out at night.

- If you like sports, play fantasy. There is no disadvantage sitting in a wheelchair.

- You are only giving your balance a workout if you are really, really frightened.

- Take no shit.

- Maybe a support group is a waste of time. Maybe you will find a new best friend. Give it a chance.

- Be patient.

- See a dietician at least once.

- Don't fight tiredness. Rest. Fighting it will haunt you later.

- Eating by yourself, with a bib and slobbering all over the place, is better than being fed.

- Rolling up to a table and sleeping on a pillow on the table is better than you think.

- Listen to music. Even if there is no physical movement, dance.

- Smile at walkers giving you advice. They have no idea.

- People in public look less at you than you think.

- Make new friends. As opposed to the old ones, they will never think about your loss.

- Do not blindly trust doctors. Nobody knows your body like you.

- X-rays can be wrong.

- Get advice from a physical therapist. Meet at least monthly.

- Many amusement parks give advantages to cripples. Take full advantage.

- Don't be a hero. Use the handicap parking.

- At first, children and dogs will fear the wheelchair. It will pass.

- Listen to audio books.

- Don't eat too much.

- Don't remove the flip-over protectors on your wheelchair until you are certain.

- Play sit-down badminton. Start off with a balloon.

- Walking is not a prerequisite to riding horses or off-roading.

- Learn self-massage.

- Stretch.

- Say, "I am in a wheelchair" to yourself over and over until it stops hurting.

- If you are home alone, create and practice your fire escape.

- Learn to use a computer. Research your condition.

- Take charge of your life. Do not expect doctors to do so.

- Once per month, pig out and eat your favorite food. Otherwise, eat healthy.

- Resist the temptation to put stickers on your wheelchair.

- Weight is an enemy. Lose it.

- If something hurts, stop. Life in a wheelchair should not be painful.

- Keep your tires at the right pressure.

- A wheelchair is not an excuse not to give or get hugs.

- Get ready to scrape your knuckles.

- Get a ride on a lawn mower.

- When traveling, especially by air, bring pills to prevent an upset stomach.

- Give people an extra chance.

- Shabby-looking ramps are usually shabby.

- If you really don't want to go, call and say you are having a "handicap problem." Works every time.

- The only person you have to improve is yourself from yesterday.

- Never accept a higher price because of your handicap.

- It is a process.

- Drop every single prejudice you hold.

- Take a refresher course in wheelchair technique yearly.

- Being terribly out of shape is simply not an option.

- Don't use your wheelchair story to break the ice.

- Don't always take the easy path.

- As it suits you, the wheelchair is a bike. Other times, it is your legs.

- Don't let the simple fact that you are in a wheelchair win you arguments.

- When getting a new wheelchair, it is OK to be giddy like a child at Christmas.

- Take care of your back. Your life will be tough without it.

- Always take neck pain seriously. See a doctor.

- A small towel shoved down between your lower back and the backrest can help with posture.

- Lie in a sofa daily. Say you are stretching your back.

- Read a medical periodical.

- If getting up and dressed is a hassle, it will not be a hassle soon.

- Be careful when rolling behind people. They tend to stop for no reason with absolutely no warning.

- Learn the rules of the major wheelchair sports.

- Have a good relationship with your wheelchair. Make it your best friend.

- The only acceptable wheelchair decoration is colored spokes.

- Slowly but surely you will enjoy the small things more.

- Have fun.

- Be up for the challenge.

- Be early to sporting events; the best wheelchair spots are usually really good, while the worst can be really bad.

- If you feel self-pity, go to a hospital. See? It's not so bad.

- Nod and acknowledge other wheelchair users.

- When people say, "no problem, we will carry you," it is usually in fact a big problem.

- Friends will react very differently. Some will barely notice, while others will obsess. Your job is to accept both. They are processing.

- Rolling around outside when it is pitch black can be a bad idea.

- Spoiling yourself because you are in a wheelchair is OK.

- Let your first big trip be to a major US city. It is accessible, and people are patient, understanding, and helpful.

- If you enjoy art, go to a museum. Having your own seat is great.

- You are now an expert in crisis management. Not many are.

- More than anything, your attitude will form your future. Form a good one!

- Circulation in your feet is important. Do stuff to get blood pumping.

- When you are put in a car, think safety.

- Avoid like the plague the word, "invalid." You aren't.

- When training, do one more.

- You must fit under your dining table. Accept no compromise.

- For all intents and purposes, your wheelchair is a toy.

- Get spoke protectors. Stay classy and get them without a logo.

- Have a daily gymnastic routine.

- Never question anyone using the handicap-designated parking. Many handicaps are invisible.

- When on a hiking trail, wear hiking boots.

- Read the Americans with Disabilities Act.

- Don't break your back. Ask for a push. Seriously, your back is important.

- When you reach a goal, get another. Never settle.

- Before transferring to a toilet, check for TP. Before.

- There is help for everything. Don't get too dependent.

- Likely, your body-temperature system has gone haywire. Get a fan.

- Don't worry.

- What you assume will be the toughest might very well be the easiest.

- Stairs, up or down, are not necessarily a problem.

- Hotels will always be less than ideal. Adapt.

- Young pets disassociate the wheelchair from any danger. Be careful.

- When in a public building, locate the fire escape.

- Don't assume people feel sad for you.

- If worse comes to worse, sit on the toilet and shower.

- With a child in your lap, don't go fast.

- Stained trousers show extra well. Wear a napkin.

- Once in a while give your cushion a deep clean. Let it air dry over night.

- Learn some tricks with your wheelchair.

- Try to develop enough strength to go up curbs.

- Don't fear going down curbs.

- If you engage in a snow-ball or water fight, prepare to lose.

- Some products targeted at us handicapped are perfect answers to questions never asked. Beware.

- Don't get a car with sporty bucket seats.

- If your back hurts from a soft bed, try elevating your legs.

- Every so often, get pushed fast to feel the wind in your hair.

- Don't settle for "good enough" with your sitting. Sit right.

- If you have an infection in your body, it might react more strongly than it did before.

- If you drive your own car, have some big towels along. Especially if it snows where you are.

- Sometimes, handrails are handy for pulling when going up a ramp.

- Take, and document, your blood pressure monthly.

- The second time is so much easier. Try.

- Since you move less, the sun can be particularly harmful. Use sunscreen.

- Learn to fall "comfortably."

- When everybody stands, like when a bride walks down the aisle, try not to lean against the backrest.

- Slow progress is progress.

- Have a plan B.

- Read *The Little Engine that Could.*

- Support stores with really good handicap-designated parking. And stay away from stores that have none.

- If you can balance on your back wheels, great. Don't flaunt it.

- If something scares you, maybe you should do it anyway.

- Don't use your legs to hold cups of hot liquid.

- Have twice the recommended amount of fire extinguishers at home. The same goes for smoke detectors.

- You can be in a wheelchair and still be the US president.

- It is not automatically OK to be late.

- With someone around to catch you, find the wheelchair tip limit.

- Offer to make dinner. Get an early start.

- Racer wheels designed for speed on hard ground generally suck on soft ground.

- When trying to help, people will mess up. Be kind.

- Don't let loved ones wear themselves out helping you.

- Do the limbo.

- Become a technical expert at your wheelchair.

- A low car is easy to get into and difficult to get out of.

- Ask for help when you need it.

- When rolling, do spurts of max speed; it is good practice.

- Before falling asleep, try some sit-ups.

- Practice carefully backing up, particularly if your wheelchair is electric.

- Practice driving on two wheels.

- Don't sit passively on the sideline; at least be an active observer.

- Changing your dreams and goals is OK.

- Try something new. Make sure you aren't alone.

- If you play wheelchair rugby and suck at it, blame the equipment.

- In elevators, be aware of children's feet.

- If your favorite store is inaccessible, tell the owner. They want your business.

- Hide your face and weep if you stop going out.

- Know, by heart, your wheelchair's weight and dimensions.

- Have at least one mirror in your home where all of you is visible.

- There are sand-friendly wheelchairs.

- Generally speaking, the less a country is accessible, the more helpful the citizens.

- Don't let a broken body turn into a broken person.

- Keep updated on stem cell research.

- Make your kitchen accessible.

- Sometimes the grass simply *is* greener on the other side. Don't let fear of the journey stop you from going.

- If your wheelchair is electric, exchange batteries before you must.

- Don't let people push you with one hand. Both or none.

- Ensure your wheelchair tracks straight.

- Get a really good pillow.

- If at all possible, don't sit in your wheelchair when cutting your hair.

- Don't repair broken wheelchair parts; replace them.

- Now and then, sleep with your feet elevated.

- Do crossword puzzles.

- Take every chance to get a foot rub, even if you don't feel it.

- Pack hand sanitizer.

- Assume you can go anywhere. You probably can.

- In the unlikely event of something not being tried before, be the first.

- Don't tread where you can't see ground.

- When mad, do dips.

- Expecting special treatment based solely on the wheelchair is bad form.

- For young children, normalcy can take forever.

- Things not working are rarely due to lack of will.

- Get going a bit earlier.

- Be absurdly creative. Almost anything is possible.

- Heavy shopping bags hanging on your wheelchair play havoc on its balance.

- Trust your legs.

- Even with no movement or support, your legs help you.

- Make great-looking food.

- Don't let temporary failure become permanent defeat.

- When merchants have no access, it is their loss.

- Sometimes the best of intentions can go wrong. Give props for trying.

- If you transfer, think first about foot placement.

- Your best is good enough. More is impossible.

- If your breaks suddenly start sucking, check your tire pressure.

- People in wheelchairs can bungee jump.

- Don't hide away from the world in your safe place.

- Traveling by air is easy. They are used to wheelchairs.

- While your rights have not shrunk, they have also not grown.

- Don't let your wheelchair become an elephant in the corner.

- When children want a ride, get the green light from a parent.

- Long, steep hills can teach lessons better not learnt.

- Wear shoes.

- At least once, watch the Paralympics in person.

- Don't abuse people's innate helpfulness.

- Put a stool in your shower.

- Lawns heal very quickly from wheelchair tracks.

- Your wheelchair is sturdier than you think.

- Lay a puzzle.

- Have, and voice, an emergency exit plan when flying.

- When it comes to wheelchair decorations, less really is more.

- Don't compromise on personal safety.

- Wipe off dirty wheels when going inside.

- Rain and snow on wood makes for slippery footing.

- Only in the gym should you try something a little heavier than you can bear.

- Your ears are extra visible. Clean them.

- Don't slouch.

- Only your personal measuring stick matters. Only you know what your best is.

- Take advantage of always having a chair along. Stop and watch something beautiful.

- Even a pro now and then smashes into stuff with the wheelchair.

- Often, backrests are adjustable. Put in the time.

- Don't underestimate yourself.

- It is highly unlikely that your hamstrings don't need stretching.

- Just because you're not running around doesn't mean you don't need water. If anything, you need more. Drink up!

- Get a desk that lowers and rises.

- Partake in all family sofa purchasing.

- When it comes to help for us cripples, it was not better back in the day. The best day ever is today.

- If you have a significant other, hold his or her hand.

- Not all rejection is discrimination.

- Get an office chair with breaks.

- Kitchen chairs with armrests are safe to be in but difficult to get into.

- Prepare lots of questions for your doctor. Be wary of the ones with all the answers.

- Sometimes young children will say mean things. They don't mean it.

- Rugs are your enemy.

- People who push you become better pushers once they have tried being pushed.

- Never ever try showing you can't walk.

- Seeing someone else in a wheelchair, you might be tempted to say, "I know what you are going through." Don't. You don't.

- Walk a dog.

- Don't be pushed by anyone in flip-flops.

- If it is safe, spend some time alone.

- Offer your lap for heavy shopping bags.

- Work hard.

- Have a large poncho.

- Don't have an abnormally high or low bed.

- Make certain your physical therapist is roughly your age.

- Don't worry about cruel words. Worry about the cruel person saying them.

- Dream big. Strive bigger.

- Invite your occupational therapist to your home.

- Know of some local wheelchair-friendly taxi services.

- Wage war on dandruff.

- Don't place your TV too high.

- Don't go to the movies if the wheelchair spot is at the very front.

- People will give you the strangest gifts. Smile and say, "Thanks."

- The biggest wheelchair obstacle is usually in your head.

- Sleep with your wheelchair close by.

- Even without arm function, you can ski. Just try.

- When on a small boat, insist on a life preserver.

- Change damp pants.

- Take a flight in a helicopter. Feel the freedom of movement.

- Let children stare.

- Help those in need.

- Don't sell yourself short.

- Think control rather than speed when crossing a street.

- Don't misuse the word "paraplegic."

- If you use special utensils, always bring them.

- Tanning your lower back is a challenge best left unchallenged.

- When meeting another wheelchair user, don't ask why they sit.

- Don't get that heavy thing way up there.

- Move around. Meet people. Do things. Don't be a hermit.

- A good physical therapist is a bit of a sadist.

- Don't take it too seriously.

- When training, wear training clothes.

- Fall asleep lying on your side. To roll over to your back, you almost don't need to be awake.

- Don't overdo it.

- The reason you are in a wheelchair is *not* the most interesting thing about you.

- Go down sidewalks perpendicular to them.

- Try sit-down water skiing.

- Don't be a martyr.

- No one will notice if you undo the top button of your pants after a big meal.

- In general, the newer the store, the wider the aisles.

- Take initiative. People will be hesitant around you.

- When a trained professional asks you to try something scary, do it.

- Changing booths are rarely accessible. Get clothes you can return.

- Lying on a big towel greatly helps people turning you in bed.

- If someone looks tired, offer your lap as a seat.

- Keep your wheelchair clean and sharp looking.

- That live show you want to attend? Just go.

- Wheelchairs are sun magnets. Be careful.

- Now and then, get new ball bearings for your wheels.

- If your chair makes a noise, something is wrong.

- When flying, insist on gate checking your wheelchair.

- A tire is not a tire. Seek quality.

- Don't hide behind your handicap.

- If you wear hats, wash them often.

- Don't have hair so long it gets tangled in your wheels.

- The length of your footrests is vital.

- A wheelchair is no hindrance to being a great parent.

- Don't open doors by ramming your feet into them.

- When a hotel claims to have "roll-in showers," don't blindly accept it. Ask for specifics.

- Avoid extremely long flights.

- Have a plan for getting back into your chair from the ground with help.

- Pack a towel.

- When you have found your favorite wheelchair brand, take a look at their accessories. Chances are they have already solved some of your problems.

- If you are nice to your wheelchair, it tends to be nice back.

- Especially when flying, massage your legs.

- When planning a trip to a vastly different climate, consult a doctor.

- Get a bed that operates electrically.

- Match your socks.

- Never be towed.

- If you say, "no," it is final. Your physical therapist may, and probably will, ignore this rule.

- Accept that ultimate comfort is unattainable. Instead of aiming for perfection, aim for continual small improvements.

- When you think of a way to improve your wheelchair, tell the manufacturer.

- Be willing to try new products.

- Your wheelchair can handle rain better than you can.

- Although there was no reason, now make a purpose.

- You must probably kill some sacred cows. Be quick.

- The difference in comfort when a wheelchair is customized for you is monumental.

- When you feel like strangling your physical therapist, remember the second word of the phrase "tough love."

- If your arms don't work, try blow darts.

- Instead of blindly backing up, roll forward a bit and turn around.

- A wheelchair is not a hindrance to finding or keeping a loving spouse.

- Now and then, sadness is OK.

- Talk to someone.

- Stubbornness way past your limitations can be costly.

- Get a good backpack.

- Sorry to say it, but just being in a wheelchair does not make you special.

- Squeaky wheels often mean underinflated wheels.

- Getting into a pool is a hassle. Being in a pool is great.

- If there is any movement whatsoever, you can drive.

- Think of other people's backs.

- When exposed to blatant discrimination, protest loudly.

- If you have space, have a side-by-side fridge and freezer.

- Sleep with an extra pillow.

- Don't use your wheelchair story to trump everyone else's story.

- Your wheelchair is not a social license to be grumpy.

- Curiosity didn't kill the cat. Answer questions, even dumb ones, with a smile.

- When meeting a child in a wheelchair, be happy and smile.

- Rotate evenly your usage of your cushions.

- Twist your back from side to side.

- Tight clothing is rarely flattering.

- Both an experienced wheelchair user and a new one can teach you something.

- Transferring with purpose minimizes fear.

- Watch TV standing up.

- Try a multitude of break levers.

- Be the boss.

- Acting like the wheelchair is no big thing makes your personality glow.

- Take your leg protectors/armrests off before transferring.

- Generally, transferring is easier in one direction. Practice the other.

- Asking for help proves strength.

- Even though walking comfort may matter little, wear nice shoes.

- Few things are less attractive than a cynic in a wheelchair.

- Keep your leg protectors/armrests clean.

- Wash your cushion cover often.

- Don't complain.

- Don't roll around with expensive stuff on your lap.

- Decide what you want to do, then find out if it is accessible. Not the other way around.

- When introducing yourself, don't explain the wheelchair. Let people ask.

- Be careful when wearing shorts. Exposed legs easily get pinched.

- If you sit at a desk all day, consider a stool for your feet.

- It is extra important for we who are in a wheelchair to stray away from our comfort zones. It is then and there we learn.

• Unexpected swelling or bruising calls for immediate care. Visit a doctor.

• Your wheelchair is made for sitting. You are not. Change position often.

• Allow other people to feel sad and to seek comfort in you without you stealing the stage.

- Sentences starting with "If I could only walk…" are forbidden.

- In a restaurant, transfer over to a booth sofa.

- You can still love and be loved. The wheelchair changes nothing.

- Driving a car without legs is actually rather simple.

- Stamina over brute strength.

- Use frustration to reach a little farther.

- Don't let an inability to tie shoes or put on socks hinder your independence.

- After a while, people will stop going above and beyond. It is a compliment.

- Take pictures. You have a new perspective.

- Don't go down steep hills face first.

- When walking all day is called for, rent an electric chair.

- If you can afford it, fly first class.

- There are pool-friendly wheelchairs.

- New rule: TV remotes may never be left up high.

- Look into wheelchair sports.

- Find, and join, a wheelchair-friendly gym.

- Go to the movies.

- Don't change your long-term goals. A wheelchair is a hiccup, not a roadblock.

- Look at how other wheelchair users do it. They are the best instructors.

- Stationary arm biking is monumentally boring. Tough. Just do it.

- When taking a swim, bring company.

- At first, absolutely every-thing will suck. Patience.

- Soak in a tub.

- Salesmen for major wheelchair companies generally want you to have the best wheelchair, not the most expensive.

- If your favorite restaurant is not wheelchair friendly, order it to go.

- Make certain you learn to roll around in bed.

- Dress with pride.

- The blame game has no winners.

- When another wheelchair user wants to tell you something, listen.

- Spend time and money on finding the perfect mattress.

- Get a laser pointer.

- Horseback ride.

- Get the best wheelchair you can afford.

- Frequent a grocery store with wide aisles.

- Stores with no wheelchair access do not want your money. Don't give it to them.

- When you push your wheelchair along, you are walking. Not rolling.

- Never play the "I'm handicapped" card.

- If your physical therapist recommends a lap belt, listen.

- If you don't want to do something, you probably shouldn't.

- Don't accept pain from the wheelchair.

- If you are taking medicine, always bring some so you can sleep away from home.

- Practice quickly getting out of your car.

- If you are getting better, remember that you now and then will plateau.

- Don't let poor stamina hinder excursions. Get in shape.

- Don't let people stress you.

- Don't be late.

- If the choice must be made, happy nurses are more valuable than happy doctors.

- When in a hospital, remember that they are there for you. Not the other way around.

- Get a good air compressor.

- For a TV dinner, put a pillow and a tray in your lap.

- If you must go down steps, go backward.

- Don't buy a used wheelchair.

- Sit in a hammock.

- When selecting an apartment, assume the elevator will work.

- When flying, bring your cushion onboard.

- During winter, wear gloves.

- Sometimes fear masquerades as discrimination. Learn when.

- Loose-fitting pants get caught in the wheels.

- Overestimate how long it might take.

- Never ever, under any circumstances, comb hair over a bald spot.

- People who say, "I know how you feel" don't. But they are trying.

- If you have an electric chair, keep it charged.

- Use professional movers not because you are handicapped, but because you are smart.

- People will underestimate you. Blow them away.

- Try to be generally positive. It will help many.

- Be ecstatic about what you have. Work like a dog for what you want.

- If you have no sense of feeling in your legs, be extra careful.

- Hardwood or tile over carpet, any day of the week.

- Make a mental note of the emergency exit when entering a new room.

- The worse your hands are, the more you need a great occupational therapist.

- Weigh yourself often.

- Modern electric wheelchairs can handle worse weather than you can.

- Don't chop firewood with an axe.

- Don't trust a wheelchair expert who is not in a wheelchair.

- Keep your tires at identical pressure.

- Drink tons of sour fruit drinks. UTIs don't mess around.

- Travel.

- Not hearing from people probably means they are scared.

- Instead of doing nothing, grab your wheels and do mini-dips.

- If you have full strength in your arms, your handicap will barely be noticeable.

- Meet a personal trainer who is wheelchair bound.

- If you can, get a car.

- Keep your back flexible.

- Practice picking stuff up off the floor.

- Boxing is often good training.

- Prepare for children asking, "Why?"

- Major US cities are extremely accessible.

- When flying, be on time.

- The United States has wheelchair-accessible taxis.

- Go to a mall. Hang out.

- If you lose friends, they are not real friends. The real friends stay.

- Unfortunately, there are plenty of jobs where a wheelchair is not a hindrance.

- Transferring out of your chair might, at first, be scary. Get over it.

- Don't accept the last row on an airplane. To lift you safely, somebody needs to stand behind you.

- Aim for the stars.

- Find a good occupational therapist. They solve problems.

- Hope.

- Daydream.

- Don't wait for divine aid. Roll up your sleeves and help yourself.

- Smile.

- Be the first one to make a cripple joke.

- Make your policy "If you don't ask, I won't tell."

- Some things you can do, but probably should not. It takes too much time.

- Don't worry, it has been done before.

- It could be so much worse.

- You can't win 'em all. Win the next one instead.

- At least once, visit New York.

- Don't hide your true emotions from loved ones. They already know.

- Think you don't need courses in wheelchair technique? Think again.

- Getting into a boat is easier than you think.

- Often, the most expensive wheelchair tie downs for your car are the best. Don't skimp.

- Have no balance? There are machines for that.

- Always pack a good book.

- Bad legs don't excuse bad manners.

- Self-pity mostly harms others.

- You are not a victim. Don't accept being treated as one.

- Just because your learning curve is steep, it doesn't mean it is short.

- Get used to steep inclines and declines. Sooner or later, they happen.

- Door sills suck. Get mini ramps.

- Pat yourself on the back. But not too hard; it hurts.

- Get frequent back rubs. Call them "medically relevant."

- Being confined to a wheelchair does not, per definition, make you "sick." Don't put up with that attitude from anybody, including yourself.

- Don't pity yourself. Mourn for a while, then get on with it.

- Don't equate being free from medicine with being healthy.

- Keep your fingernails short and your hands moisturized. You will use them much.

- Don't remove the helpers' handlebars on your backrest. They will be used.

- Get a comfortable cushion. You sit a lot.

- Even if you have no hope of walking, train your legs.

- If there is something you want to do, tell someone. You can do anything.

- Remember, your rights are intact.

- Posture, posture, posture.

- If push comes to shove, you will fall out of your chair. You must be extremely unlucky for it to hurt.

- If you can, avoid electric wheelchairs. They make you feel sicker than you are.

- Never give up.

- Give your wheelchair a name.

- Keep a diary.

- If you are getting better, measure your achievements monthly. Progress is difficult to spot.

- When you can, practice getting comfortable on the floor. Eventually you will fall..

- Being in a wheelchair is a perfect excuse not to vacuum.

- Find at least one medical professional you trust. Ask questions.

- Believe it or not, you are lucky.

- Get new tires for your wheelchair before you are forced to.

- Keep your wheelchair lubed.

- When you absolutely must trust your wheelchair brakes, don't.

- Being out-of-control drunk and in a wheelchair is not a good idea.

- Get used to saying, "Don't touch my chair!"

- Eat a multivitamin.

- Don't hurt the ones you love.

- One would think cats would move out of your way. Not always true.

- Laugh.

- Don't get a wheelchair more advanced than you can handle.

- There is no shame in using the foot stands indoors.

- Don't compromise on your principles. But be willing to reconsider.

- Your mood will crash. Just accept it, but find a cure. Mine is cake.

- Celebrate your "rebirth-day" in style. Have cake.

17887298R00085

Made in the USA
Charleston, SC
05 March 2013